Fruits Crochet

Fruit Amigurumi Tutorial

Easy to Follow Instructions for Beginners

Copyright © 2020

All rights reserved.

DEDICATION

The author and publisher have provided this e-book to you for your personal use only. You may not make this e-book publicly available in any way. Copyright infringement is against the law. If you believe the copy of this e-book you are reading infringes on the author's copyright, please notify the publisher at: https://us.macmillan.com/piracy

Contents

Fruit Crochet Coasters Pattern 3

Amigurumi Strawberry Crochet Pattern 19

Lemon or Lime Wedge Crochet Pattern 28

Bunch of Grapes Crochet Pattern 33

Banana Crochet Pattern 46

Chilli Billy Crochet Pattern 50

Tiny Carrot Crochet Pattern 56

Fruit Crochet Coasters Pattern

This pattern uses US terms and stitches include double crochet (dc), slip stitch (sl st), and chain (ch).

Supplies0

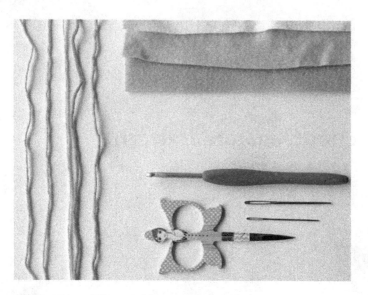

Yarn (I used Drops Paris cotton)

Crochet hook (4mm)

Darning needle for sewing in the ends

Felt

Sewing needle

Sewing thread (not shown)

Scissors

Crochet the Potholder

Step 1

Start with your white yarn. Begin by making a magic circle, and secure with a stitch.

Step 2

Chain 2, then work 11dc into the ring, for a total of 12 stitches.

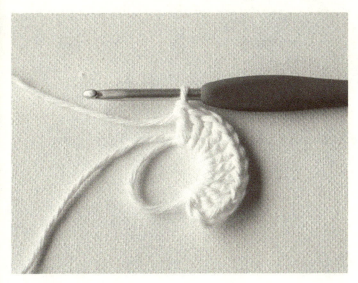

Cut the yarn, pull through the loop on your hook, and close the magic circle by pulling on the bottom yarn tail.

Close the circle by threading your yarn tail, and inserting the needle from front to back through the first dc you made, skipping the chain 2.

Insert your needle through the back loop of the last dc you made.

Sew in both ends.

Step 3

Grab your orange yarn, and start with a slip knot on your hook.

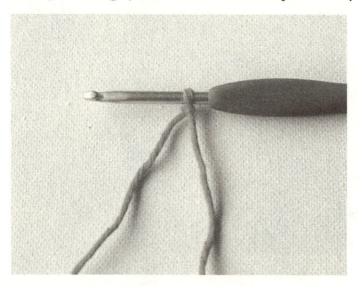

Start by making a dc into your white circle. This way of starting a round is called a standing stitch. We're going to start all of our new colours like this from now on.

Work 2dc into every stitch around. Your stitch total is now 24. Join with a slip stitch in the first dc.

Step 4

Chain 3, then work 2dc into the next stitch. Work *1dc, inc* around (inc means increase; work 2 stitches into one stitch). Join with a slip stitch to the top chain of your beginning chain 3. Your stitch total is now 36.

Step 5

Chain 3, then work 1dc into the next stitch, and 2dc into the stitch after that. Work *2dc, inc* around. Join with a slip stitch. Your stitch total is now 48.

Step 6

Chain 3, then work 2dc into the next two stitches, and 2dc into the stitch after that. Work *3dc, inc* around. Your stitch total is now 60. Cut the yarn, and join the round like you did with the white circle. Sew in the ends.

Step 7

Join your white yarn like you did with the orange yarn. Work *4dc, inc* around. Join with a slip stitch. Your stitch total is now 72. Cut the yarn, and join the round like you did with the white circle. Sew in the ends.

Step 8

Join your orange yarn like you did before. Work *5dc, inc* around. Join with a slip stitch. Your stitch total is now 84. Cut the yarn, and join the round like you did with the white circle. Sew in the ends.

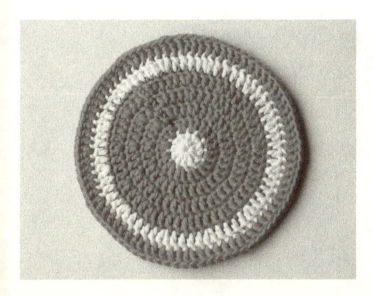

Step 9

We're now going to crochet the wedges by using surface slip stitches. Grab your white yarn, and pull it to the front from the center of your piece. Slip stitch your way up to the second white round. Cut the yarn and sew in the ends. Repeat this 5 more times.

Sew on the Back

Step 1

We're going to sew on a piece of felt, to give our potholder a finished look, and to make it more rugged. Cut out a piece of felt that is the same size as your crochet piece.

Step 2

Put your crochet piece on top of your felt. Grab some sewing thread and your sewing needle, and attach the felt to the crochet piece using a blanket stitch.

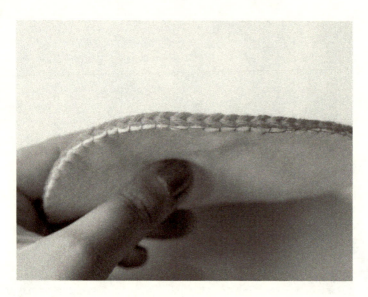

Step 3

Sew in the ends.

Amigurumi Strawberry Crochet Pattern

Finished Size: 2" x 1.25" (including stems)

Supplies:

Worsted weight yarn in red, white & green

Size G (4.0 mm) Crochet Hook

Tapestry Needle

Scissors

Poly-fil

Abbreviations (US Terms):

BLO - Back Loop Only

Ch - Chain

Sc - Single Crochet

Sc2tog - Single Crochet 2 Together

Sl st - Slip Stitch

Important Notes:

-All joins are made with a sl st.

-Your first stitch is always worked in the same space as the ch 1.

-Sc2tog counts as 1 sc.

-Gauge is not important for this pattern just be sure to work your stitches tight so your stuffing doesn't show through.

Row 1: Ch 4, sc in 2nd ch from hook, sc in next, 3 sc in last.

Rotate piece to the right so you can work on the opposite side of the foundation chain.

Sc in next, 2 sc in next. Join. (8 sc)

Row 2: Ch 1, 2 sc in first, sc in 2. 2 sc in each of the next 2, sc in 2, 2 sc in last. Join. (12 sc)

Row 3-7: Ch 1, sc in each around. Join. (12 sc)

Before moving on, use white yarn to stitch on little seeds.

Row 8: In BLO: Ch 1, *Sc in 2, sc2tog.* Repeat *to* around. Join. (9 sc)

Fasten off leaving a long end to sew your opening shut.

Now, the final step is adding the little green stems. Cut 3-5 strands of green yarn about 4" in length, then use your needle to slip each piece through the top of the strawberry. Tie each piece on with a knot, knot a 2nd time to secure yarn. Trim to about an inch in length.

Cherry on top Cupcake Crochet Pattern

Fruits Crochet

Finished size: 2.5"W x 3.75"H (with cherry)

Supplies:

Worsted Weight Yarn in red for the cherry and 2 choice colors for the cupcake & frosting

Optional: Additional yarn in various colors for sprinkles.

Size G (4.0 mm) Crochet Hook

Tapestry needle

Stitch marker

Scissors

Polyfil

Optional: Small piece of cardboard

Abbreviations (US Terms):

BLO - Black Loop Only

Ch - Chain

Dc - Double Crochet

Fphdc - Front Post Half Double Crochet

Hdc - Half Double Crochet

Sc - Single Crochet

Sl st - Slip Stitch

Important Notes:

-Ch 1 does not count as a stitch.

-All joins are made with a sl st.

-Sc2tog counts as one sc.

-Your first stitch of each row will always be worked in the same space as your ch 1 or ch 2.

Cupcake

With Cake color:

Row 1: Magic circle, ch 1, 6 sc in circle. Join. (6 sc)

Row 2: Ch 1, 2 sc in each around. Join. (12 sc)

Row 3: Ch 1, *sc, 2 sc in next.* Repeat *to* around. Join. (18 sc)

Row 4: Ch 1, *sc in 2, 2 sc in next.* Repeat *to* around. Join. (24 sc)

Row 5: Ch 1, *sc in 3, 2 sc in next.* Repeat *to* around. Join. (30 sc)

Sew in your beginning end.

Optional: If you would like your cupcake to stand up perfectly, trace the circle you've made onto a piece of cardboard. Cut out the cardboard circle slightly smaller than the traced circle and then place the piece of cardboard into the bottom of the cupcake. The cupcake will stand without the cardboard bottom but this makes for a very nice flat bottom.

Row 6: In BLO: Ch 1, hdc in each around. Join. (30 hdc)

Row 7-11: Ch 1, *hdc, fphdc around next.* Repeat *to* around. Join. (15 hdc, 15 fphdc)

Fasten off.

Place a stitch marker in the front loop on the first hdc you made on row 11.

With Frosting color:

Join with a sl st in the back loop of any stitch.

Row 12: In BLO: Ch 1, sc in each around. Join. (30 sc)

Row 13: Ch 1, *sc in 8, sc2tog.* Repeat *to* around. Join. (27 sc)

Row 14: Ch 1, *sc in 7, sc2tog.* Repeat *to* around. Join. (24 sc)

Row 15: Ch 1, *sc in 6, sc2tog.* Repeat *to* around. Join. (21 sc)

Row 16: Ch 1, *sc in 5, sc2tog.* Repeat *to* around. Join. (18 sc)

Row 17: Ch 1, *sc in 4, sc2tog.* Repeat *to* around. Join. (15 sc)

Begin to stuff your cupcake and continue to do so as you go.

Now is also a good time to start stitching on sprinkles if you would like them.

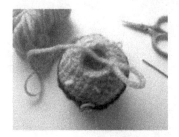

Row 18: Ch 1, *sc in 3, sc2tog.* Repeat *to* around. Join. (12 sc)

Row 19: Ch 1, *sc in 2, sc2tog.* Repeat *to* around. Join. (9 sc)

Fasten off leaving a long end for sewing, sew hole shut and sew in end.

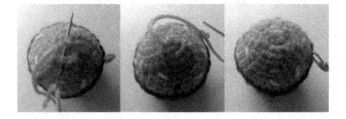

With Frosting color:

Hold the cupcake with the frosting top facing you.

Join with a sl st in the space your stitch marker is in, you can now remove the stitch marker.

Row 20: Ch 2, 2 dc in first. 3 dc in next and in each around. Join.

Fasten off and sew in ends.

Cherry

With Red:

Row 1: Magic circle, ch 1, 6 sc in circle. Join. (6 sc)

Row 2: Ch 1, *sc, 2 sc in next.* Repeat *to* around. Join. (9 sc)

Row 3: Ch 1, *sc in 2, 2 sc in next.* Repeat *to* around. Join. (12 sc)

Now is a good time to secure your beginning end.

If you want a stem on your cherry pull this end through to the right side of the cherry after securing it. Tie a knot as close as you can to the cherry and tie another knot about an inch or two away from the cherry. Trim.

Row 4: Ch 1, sc in each around. Join. (12 sc)

Row 5: Ch 1, *sc in 2, sc2tog.* Repeat *to* around. Join. (9 sc)

Row 6: Ch 1, *sc, sc2tog.* Repeat *to* around. Join. (6 sc)

Fasten off leaving a long end to sew the cherry to the top of the cupcake.

Sew cherry to the cupcake then sew in your end.

Lemon or Lime Wedge Crochet Pattern

Finished Size: 2" x 1.25"

Supplies:

Worsted weight yarn

   -For Lime: White, Light Green & Dark Green

   -For Lemon: White, Light Yellow & Dark Yellow

Size G Crochet Hook

Tapestry Needle

Scissors

Poly-fil

Fruits Crochet

Abbreviations (US Terms):

Ch - Chain

Sc - Single Crochet

Sl st - Slip Stitch

Important Notes:

-All joins are made with a sl st.

-Your first stitch is always worked in the same space as the ch 1.

-Stitches listed between the following brackets [ ] indicate a group of stitches that need to be worked into the same space.

With White:

Row 1: Magic circle, ch 1, 6 sc in circle. Join. (6 sc)

Fasten off leaving a long end (about 12") for using later.

With Lighter Color:

Join with a sl st.

Row 2: Ch 1, 2 sc in each around. Join. (12 sc)
Row 3: Ch 1, *sc, 2 sc in next.* Repeat *to* around. Join. (18 sc)

Fasten off.

With White:

Join with a sl st.

Row 4: Ch 1, *sc in 2, 2 sc in next.* Repeat *to* around. Join. (24 sc)

Fasten off, sew in ends except for the end indicated to leave long, set aside.

(Peel)

With Darker Color:

Row 1: Ch 8, sc in 2nd ch from hook, sc in 5, 3 sc in last.

Rotate piece to the right so you can work on the opposite side of the foundation chain.

Sc in next 5, 2 sc in last. Join. (16 sc)

Row 2: Ch 1, 3 sc in first, sc in 6, [3 sc, ch 2, sl st to top of sc] in next, 3 sc in next. Sc in 6, [3 sc, ch 2, sl st to top of sc] in last. Join. (24 sc)

Fasten off leaving a long end for sewing.

Now holding together the lighter colored piece to the peel with the wrong sides facing each other, use your needle to sew the edges of the pieces together. I chose to only sew through one loop on the light side, this is optional. Stuff as you go but do not over stuff.

Next, use the white long end to create the different sections of the lemon/lime.

Sew in ends.

Bunch of Grapes Crochet Pattern

Supplies

Bernat Blanket Yarn in colors: White, Taupe, Race Car Red, Carrot Orange, Go Go Green, and Pow Purple

Size N/P (10.0 mm) crochet hook (I used Clover Amour)

Plastic Yarn Needle

Non-toxic puffy paint in black

Abbreviations (US Terms)

Ch: chain

sl st: slip stitch

SC: single crochet

SC2TOG: Single crochet two together

DC: Double crochet

Bobble stitch (bobble): YO, insert hook and pull yarn through st from previous row, YO, pull through 2 loops on the hook, YO, insert hook into same stitch and pull through, YO, pull through 2, YO, insert hook into same stitch and pull through, YO, Pull through 2, YO, Pull through the 4 remaining loops on the hook.

BLO: Back loop only

RSC (crab stitch): Reverse single crochet

Pattern Notes:

Ch sts at the beginning of rows or rounds do not count as a stitch.

When working in rounds, the last st of a round is attached to the first st of the same round with a sl st.

Gauge is not important for the finished product, however, tight stitches help the yarn hold its shape better. If you are having trouble getting your stitches tight enough, use a smaller crochet hook.

Instructions:

Basket (using color 'Taupe')

Ch 9

Round 1: Starting in second ch from hook, SC down the ch. Work 3 SC in the last ch st and continue to SC down the back of the ch. when you reach the first ch st, work 2 more SC into that stitch (18)

Round 2: Ch 1, 2 SC, SC in next 6, 2 SC in next 3, SC in next 6, 2 SC in next 2 (24)

Round 3: Ch 1, 2 SC, SC in next 9, 2 SC in next 3, SC in next 9, 2 SC in next 2 (30)

Round 4: Ch 1, 2 SC in next 2, SC in next 10, 2 SC in next 5, SC in next 10, 2 SC in next 3 (40)

Round 5: Ch 1, 2 SC in next 2, SC in next 15, 2 SC in next 5, SC in next 15, 2 SC in next 3 (50)

Round 6-7: Ch 1, SC around (50)

Round 8: Ch 1, in BLO, SC around (50)

Round 9-15: Ch 1, SC around (50) Tie off.

Basket Handle

Ch 26

Row 1: SC in second ch from hook. SC across (25) Turn

Row 2-3: SC across. (25) Do not tie off yet

With a sl st (on the inside of the basket) attach one end of the handle in sts 12-14 of round 15. Cut and tie off yarn. Attach the other end of the handle in sts 37-39. Do not tie off. Continue to crab stitch (RSC) around the rim of the basket and handle. Attach to the first RSC with sl st. Tie off yarn. Attach with sl st to the other side of the handle and RSC around. Attach to the first RSC of the round. Tie off and weave in ends.

Watermelon Half (Race Car Red, Go Go Green, White)

For the rind: Start with Magic Circle (in 'Go Go Green')

Round 1: Ch 1, work 8 SC into magic circle

Round 2: Ch 1, 2 SC in each st around (16)

Round 3, Ch 1, *2 SC, SC, repeat from *around (24)

Round 4-6: Ch 1, SC around (24). Cut and tie off yarn

For the fruit: Start with Magic Circle (in 'Race Car Red')

Round 1: Ch 1, work 8 SC into magic circle

Round 2: Ch 1, 2 SC in each st around (16)

Round 3: Ch 1, *2 SC, SC, repeat from *around (24)

Round 4: *switch to color 'White', sl st around row 3 (24)

Place this circle in the rind portion of the watermelon and, working through BLO of the white and both loops of the green rind, sl st around to attach them. Tie off and weave in ends.

Decorate seeds with non-toxic puffy paint

Grapes (Pow Purple, Go Go Green)

Grape Bunch (Pow Purple-make 2)

Ch 10

Row 1: Start in third ch from the hook, *bobble, SC, repeat from * across (4 bobbles, 4 SC)

Row 2: Ch 1, SC2TOG, SC in 4, SC2TOG (6)

Row 3: Ch 2, *bobble, SC, repeat from * across (3 bobbles, 3 SC)

Row 4: Ch 1, SC2TOG, SC in 2, SC2TOG (4)

Row 5: Ch 2, *bobble, SC, repeat from *across (2 bobbles, 2 SC)

Row 6: Ch 1, SC2TOG across (2)

Row 7: Ch 1, bobble, sc

 For the first half Ch 1 and SC around the raw edge working one st into each row. *For the second half* place the wrong side of each grape half together and sl st around working through both pieces. This will create a 3 dimensional bunch of grapes

Leaf: Attach the color Go Go Green to the top of the bunch 1 with sl st. Ch 6. Working in the second ch from the hook: sl st, SC, DC, DC, SC. Now working along the back side of the chain: Ch 1, SC, DC, DC,SC, sl st. This will bring you back to the point of the leaf. Tie off yarn and weave in ends.

Vine: Attach the color Go Go Green in the same stitch as the leaf. Ch 8. Start in the second ch from the hook. Work 3 SC into each ch stitch to create a spiral. When you reach the beginning of the ch, tie off and weave in ends.

Orange Juice (Carrot Orange, White)

Start with Magic Circle (in 'Carrot Orange')

Round 1: Work 6 SC into magic circle. Pull tight (6)

Round 2: Ch 1, 2 SC in each st around (12)

Round 3: Ch 1, in BLO-SC around (12)

Round 4-11: Ch 1, SC around (12)

Round 12: *Switch to 'White'* Ch 1, SC around (12)

Round 13: Ch 1, *SC2TOG, SC, repeat from * around (6)

Round 14: Ch 1, *SC2TOG, SC, repeat from * around (3)-This will essentially "close" the top of the bottle without actually stitching it shut

Round 15: Ch 1, 2 SC in each st around (6). Tie off.

To make the bottom rim of the bottle, attach 'White' with a slip stitch to the front loop of round 2. Sl st around. Tie off and weave in ends.

Orange Crochet Pattern

Fruits Crochet

Using green yarn make a magic circle.

Rnd 1: 5 sc in magic circle, sl st to beg st to join (5 sc).

Change to orange yarn:

Rnd 2: 2 sc in each st, sl ,sl st to beg st to join (10 sc).

Rnd 3: 2 sc in 1st st, sc 1, repeat around, sl st to beg st to join (15 sc).

Rnd 4: 2 sc in 1st st, sc in next 2 sts, repeat around, sl st to beg st to join (20 sc).

Rnd 5: 2 sc in 1st st, sc in next 3 sts, repeat around, sl st to beg st to join (25 sc).

Rnd 6: 2 sc in 1st st, sc in next 4 sts, repeat around, sl st to beg st to join (30 sc).

Rnd 7: 2 sc in 1st st, sc in next 5 sts, repeat around, sl st to beg st to join (35 sc).

Rnd 8: 2 sc in 1st st, sc in next 6 sts, repeat around, sl st to beg st to join (40 sc).

Rnd 9-11: sc around (40 sc).

Rnd 13: 1 dec, sc in next 6 sts, repeat around, sl st to beg st to join (35 sc).

Rnd 14: 1 dec, sc in next 5 sts, repeat around, sl st to beg st to join (30 sc).

Rnd 15: 1 dec, sc in next 4 sts, repeat around, sl st to beg st to join (25 sc).

Rnd 16: 1 dec, sc in next 3 sts, repeat around, sl st to beg st to join (20 sc).

Rnd 17: 1 dec, sc in next 2 sts, repeat around, sl st to beg st to join (15 sc).

Rnd 18: 1 dec, sc in next st, repeat around, sl st to beg st to join, fasten off (10 sc).

Change to green yarn:

Rnd 19: dec around, sl st to beg st to join (5 sc)

Fasen off & sew tog.

Leaf:

Ch 10, sl st in 2nd ch, sc in next st, hdc in next st, dc in next st, tr in next st, dc in next st, hdc in next st, sc in next st, sl st in last st, ch 2.

Working up the opposite side:

sl st into 2nd ch, sl st into next st, sc in next st, hdc in next st, dc in next st, tr in next st, dc in next st, hdc in next st, sc in next st, sl st in next st, sl st to 1st, fasten off.

Stem:

Ch 7, sl st in 2nd ch & in next 5 ch, fasen off.

Sew leaf & stem to top of orange.

Banana Crochet Pattern

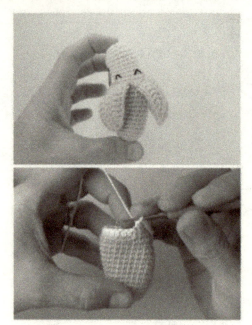

Materials:

Yellow and white yarn

Crochet hook

Needle

Scissors

Stuff

Abbreviations:

sc: single crochet

ch: chain

inc: increase

dec: decrease

CC: chenge color

BLO: back loop only

F/O: Fasten Off

Note: Working in continuous round

Banana:

Using yellow

R1: ch 2, starting from second chain from hook 6 sc

R2: inc, rep 6x (12)

R3: sc around

R4: sc, inc, rep 6x (18)

R5: sc around

R6: 8 sc, inc, rep 2x (20)

R7-9: sc around

CC to white

R10: work in BLO, sc around (20)

R11-15: sc around

R16: 8 sc, dec, rep 2x (18)

R17: sc around

R18: dec, sc, rep 6x (12)

R19: sc around

Stuff

R20: dec, rep 6x (6)

F/O

Banana Peel:

Using yellow

We will divide the peel to be 2. The first side's started from 1st-10th stitches of R10 of banana, and the second side started from 11th-20th stitches.

R1: Start working in first front loop of 10th round of banana, 10 sc, ch1, turn

R2-6: 10 sc, ch1, turn (10)

R7: dec, 6sc, dec, ch1, turn (8)

R8: dec, 4sc, dec, ch1, turn (6)

R9: dec, 2sc, dec, ch1, turn (4)

R10: 2dec, ch1, turn (2)

R11: dec (1)

F/O

Continue making the second side of peel. Repeat the steps above.

Chilli Billy Crochet Pattern

Size: Chilli Billy is approximately 5" (12 cm) tall.

You will need:

3 mm crochet hook

Scissors

3 mm knitting needle (or thereabouts)

Yarn needle

Oddments of Light Worsted Weight (DK/8ply) yarn in Red and Green

2 x 6 mm black plastic safety eyes

30 cm long Black pipe cleaner

The Pattern:

Make 1 piece, starting at tail. Working in continuous spiral rounds.

With Red yarn make 2 ch.

Rnd 1: 3 sc in second ch from hook. (3 sts)

Rnd 2: 2 sc in each of next 3 st. (6 sts)

Rnd 3: sc in each st around.

Rnd 4: [sc in next st, 2 sc in next st] 3 times. (9 sts)

Rnds 5-6: sc in each st around. (2 rounds)

Rnd 7: [sc in each of next 2 st, 2 sc in next st] 3 times. (12 sts)

Rnds 8-10: sc in each st around. (3 rounds)

Rnd 11: [sc in each of next 3 st, 2 sc in next st] 3 times. (15 sts)

Rnds 12-21: sc in each st around. (10 rounds)

Stuff chilli, continue stuffing as you go

Rnd 22: [sc in each of next 3 st, dec] 3 times. (12 sts)

Rnds 23-25: sc in each st around. (3 rounds)

Insert safety eyes between Rnds 20 and 21, spacing them 3 stitches apart.

Change to Green yarn.

Rnd 26: sc in each st around.

Rnd 27: working in back loops only: sc in each st around.

Rnd 28: dec 6 times. (6 sts)

Stalk: Slst to next st, 6 ch, sc in second ch from hook, sc in next ch, Slst in each of next 3 ch, Slst to next st on top of chilli.

Fasten off, leaving a long yarn tail for finishing. Thread yarn tail onto yarn needle, pick up front loop only of remaining 6 stitches. Pull tight to close the hole. Weave in the yarn end.

With Green yarn embroider a small 'V' just below the eyes for the mouth.

To make the leaves: Holding chilli right way up, insert hook into any leftover front loop from Rnd 27 – picture (a). Pull up a loop of Green yarn, 3 ch, Slst in same loop as join, Slst in next st, *(Slst, 3 ch, Slst) in next st, repeat from * to end 4 more times. (6 picots made)

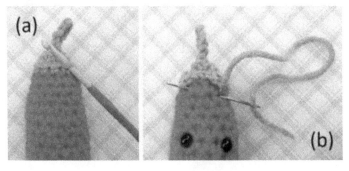

Fasten off, leaving a long yarn tail for finishing. Thread yarn tail onto yarn needle and sew the tip of each picot to the chilli – picture (b).

Cut the pipe cleaner in half and bend over the tips to create blunt ends.

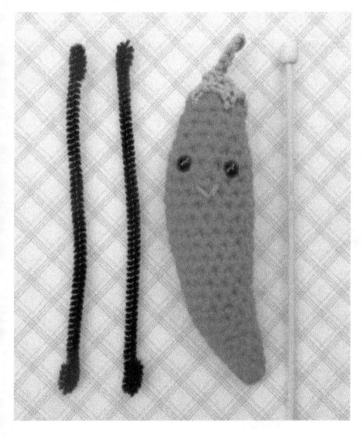

Insert the 3 mm knitting needle from side to side between Rnds 10 and 11 – picture (c). Wiggle the needle around a bit to make the hole big enough. Insert one of the pipe cleaner halves into the hole created by the knitting needle – picture (d).

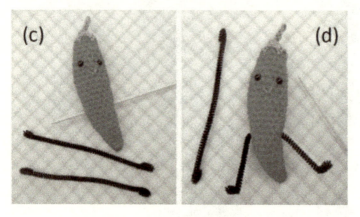

Bend the legs into shape.

Repeat the above process in between Rnds 16 and 17 for the arms.

Fruits Crochet

Tiny Carrot Crochet Pattern

Finished Size: 2.25" (with stems)

Supplies:

Worsted Weight Yarn in orange & green

Size G (4.0 mm) Crochet Hook

Tapestry Needle

Scissors

Poly-fil

Abbreviations (US Terms):

BLO - Back Loop Only

Ch - Chain

Sc - Single Crochet

Sc2tog - Single Crochet 2 Together

Sl st - Slip Stitch

Important Notes:

-All joins are made with a sl st.

-Your first stitch is always worked in the same space as the ch 1.

-Sc2tog counts as one sc.

-This pattern uses the Magic Circle, if you do not know how to make a magic circle you can learn with my quick video here: https://youtu.be/64O9WVJucFA

Row 1: Magic circle, ch 1, 6 sc in circle. Join. (6 sc)

Row 2: Ch 1, *2 sc, sc in 2.* Repeat *to* around. Join. (8 sc)

If you haven't already, sew in your beginning end.

Row 3-7: Ch 1, sc in each around. Join. (8 sc)

Stuff carrot before moving on.

Row 8: In BLO: *Sc2tog.* Repeat *to* around. Join. (4 sc)

Fasten off leaving a long end, sew top of carrot shut.

Now using green yarn, cut 3 strands about 4" in length. Use your needle to add each strand to the top of the carrot then knot all three strands together and trim to an inch or so in length.

www.ingramcontent.com/pod-product-compliance
Lightning Source LLC
LaVergne TN
LVHW041609111224
798880LV00009B/390